SRI RAMANA MAHARSHI'S Words OF Grace

WHO AM I?   SELF-ENQUIRY   SPIRITUAL INSTRUCTION

SRI RAMANASRAMAM
TIRUVANNAMALAI
INDIA

WORDS OF GRACE (English).
Original in Tamil: *Aruṇ Mozhitthoguppu* by Bhagavan Sri Ramana
Maharshi
Translated by Arthur Osborne

© Sri Ramanasramam
 Tiruvannamalai

First Edition	:	*1969*
Second Edition	:	*1978*
Third Edition	:	*1996 (5000 copies)*
Fourth Edition	:	*2005 (2000)*
Fifth Edition	:	*2007 (2000)*
Sixth Edition	:	*2008 (2000)*
Seventh Edition	:	*2010 (2000)*
Eighth Edition	:	*2013*
Ninth Edition	:	*2015 (2000)*
Tenth Edition	:	2017
2000 copies		

CC No: 1083

ISBN: 978-81-88018-03-1

Price: ₹ 40

Published by:
V.S. Ramanan
President
SRI RAMANASRAMAM
Tiruvannamalai 606 603
Tamil Nadu, INDIA
Email : *ashram@sriramanamaharshi.org*
Web : *www.sriramanamaharshi.org*

Printed by:
Sudarsan Graphics Private Limited
Chennai 600 017, INDIA

PREFATORY NOTE

The Asramam has published the three well-known works of Sri Bhagavan, namely *Who Am I?*, *Self-Enquiry* and *Spiritual Instruction* in Tamil in the form of a small volume. An English version of it is now issued for the benefit of devotees who do not know Tamil.

Who am I? (நான் யார்?) is a connected exposition of the replies given by Sri Bhagavan to certain questions put to Him by Sivaprakasam Pillai. *Self-Enquiry* (விசார சங்கிரகம்) is a similar exposition of the replies given to the questions put by Gambhiram Seshayya. *Spiritual Instruction* (உபதேச மஞ்சரி) contains the questions put by Natananandar and Sri Bhagavan's replies.

It is at the request of many western devotees that an essay form of *Who Am I?* and *Self-Enquiry* has been retained in this edition.

PUBLISHER

PREFATORY NOTE

[illegible] has published the three well known works of Bhagavan [illegible] and [illegible] in Tamil in the Original [illegible] volume. An English [illegible] now issued for [illegible] devotees who do not know Tamil.

[illegible] is a connected exposition of the [illegible] by Sri Bhagavan [illegible] questions put to Him [illegible] Pillai [illegible] is a similar [illegible] given to the questions put by [illegible]

[illegible] that an essay [illegible] has been retained in this edition.

PUBLISHER

CONTENTS

CONTENTS

Bhagavan Sri Ramana Maharshi
(1879 – 1950)

Thou dost root out the ego of those who meditate on Thee in the Heart, Oh Arunachala!

— *Arunachala Aksharamanamalai* v. 1

Who Am I?

I
WHO AM I?

EVERY living being longs always to be happy, untainted by sorrow; and everyone has the greatest love for himself, which is solely due to the fact that happiness is his real nature. Hence, in order to realise that inherent and untainted happiness, which indeed he daily experiences when the mind is subdued in deep sleep, it is essential that he should know himself. For obtaining such knowledge the enquiry, 'Who am I?' in quest of the Self is the best means.

'WHO AM I?' I am not this physical body, nor am I the five organs[1] of sense perception; I am not the five organs of external activity[2], nor am I the five vital forces,[3] nor am I even the thinking mind. Neither am I that unconscious state of nescience which retains merely the subtle *vasanas* (latencies of the mind), while being free from the functional activity of the sense-organs and the mind, and being unaware of the existence of the objects of sense-perception.

Therefore, summarily rejecting all the above-mentioned physical adjuncts and their functions, saying 'I am not this: no,

---

[1] The eye, ear, nose, tongue, and skin, with their respective corresponding functions of sight, hearing, smell, taste and touch.

[2] The vocal organs that articulate speech and produce sound, hands and feet that govern the movements of the physical body, anus that excretes faecal matter, and the genital organ which yields pleasure.

[3] Which control respiration, digestion and assimilation, circulation of blood, perspiration, and excretion.

nor am I this, nor this' — that which then remains separate and alone by itself, that pure Awareness is what I am. This Awareness self is by its very nature *Sat-Chit-Ananda*, (Being-Consciousness-Bliss).

If the mind, which is the instrument of knowledge and is the basis of all activity, subsides, the perception of the world as an objective reality ceases. Unless the illusory perception of the serpent in the rope ceases, the rope on which the illusion is formed is not perceived as such.[4] Similarly, unless the illusory nature of the perception of the world as an objective reality ceases, the vision of the true nature of the Self, on which the illusion is formed, is not obtained.

The mind is a unique power *(sakti)* in the Atman whereby thoughts occur to one. On scrutiny as to what remains after eliminating all thoughts, it will be found that there is no such thing as mind apart from thought. So then, thoughts themselves constitute the mind.

Nor is there any such thing as the physical world apart from and independent of thought. In deep sleep there are no thoughts: nor is there the world. In the wakeful and dream states thoughts are present, and there is also the world. Just as the spider draws out the thread of the cobweb from within itself and withdraws it again into itself, in the same way the mind projects the world out of itself and absorbs it back into itself.

The world is perceived as an apparent objective reality when the mind is externalized, thereby forsaking its identity with the Self. When the world is thus perceived, the true nature of the Self is not revealed: conversely, when the Self is realized, the world ceases to appear as an objective reality.

---

[4] This analogy is based on a traditional story of a man who sees a rope in the twilight and mistakes it for a serpent and is therefore afraid without cause.

By a steady and continuous investigation into the nature of the mind, the mind is transformed into *That* to which the 'I' refers; and that is in fact the Self. Mind has necessarily to depend for its existence on something gross; it never subsists by itself. It is this mind that is otherwise called the subtle body, ego, *jiva* or soul.

That which arises in the physical body as 'I' is the mind. If one enquires whence the 'I' thought in the body arises in the first instance, it will be found that it is from *hrdayam*[5] or the Heart. That is the source and stay of the mind. Or again, even if one merely continuously repeats to oneself inwardly 'I-I' with the entire mind fixed thereon, that also leads one to the same source.

The first and foremost of all the thoughts that arise in the mind is the primal 'I'-thought. It is only after the rise or origin of the 'I'-thought that innumerable other thoughts arise. In other words, only after the first personal pronoun, 'I', has arisen, do the second and third personal pronouns ('you, he', etc.) occur to the mind; and they cannot subsist without the former.

Since every other thought can occur only after the rise of the 'I'-thought and since the mind is nothing but a bundle of thoughts, it is only through the enquiry 'Who am I?' that the mind subsides. Moreover, the integral 'I'-thought, implicit in such enquiry, having destroyed all other thoughts, is itself finally destroyed or consumed, just as the stick used for stirring the burning funeral pyre is consumed.

Even when extraneous thoughts sprout up during such enquiry, do not seek to complete the rising thought but instead, deeply enquire within, 'To whom has this thought occurred?'

---

[5] The word '*hrdayam*' consists of two syllables, 'hrt' and 'ayam', (centre-this) which signify 'I am the Heart'.

No matter how many thoughts thus occur to you, if you would with acute vigilance enquire immediately as and when each individual thought arises to whom it has occurred, you would find it is to 'me'. If then you enquire 'Who am I?' the mind gets introverted and the rising thought also subsides. In this manner as you persevere more and more in the practice of Self-enquiry, the mind acquires increasing strength and power to abide in its Source.

It is only when the subtle mind is externalized through the activity of the intellect and the sense-organs that gross name and form constituting the world appear. When, on the other hand, the mind stays firmly in the Heart, they recede and disappear. Restraint of the out-going mind and its absorption in the Heart is known as introversion (*antarmukha-drishti*). The release of the mind and its emergence from the Heart is known as extroversion (*bahirmukha-drishti*).

If in this manner the mind becomes absorbed in the Heart, the ego or 'I', which is the centre of the multitude of thoughts, finally vanishes and pure Consciousness or Self, which subsists during all the states of the mind, alone remains resplendent. It is this state, where there is not the slightest trace of the 'I'-thought, that is the true Being of oneself. And that is called Quiescence or *Mouna* (Silence).

This state of mere inherence in pure Being is known as the Vision of Wisdom. Such inherence means and implies the entire subsidence of the mind in the Self. Nothing other than this and no psychic powers of the mind, such as thought reading, telepathy and clairvoyance, can be Wisdom.

Atman alone exists and is real. The threefold reality of world, individual soul, and God is, like the illusory appearance of silver in the mother of pearl, an imaginary creation in the Atman. They appear and disappear simultaneously. The Self alone is the world, the 'I' and God. All that exists is but the manifestation of the Supreme.

For the subsidence of mind there is no other means more effective and adequate than Self-enquiry. Even though by other means the mind subsides, that is only apparently so; it will rise again.

For instance, the mind subsides by the practice of *pranayama* (restraint and control of breath and vital forces); yet such subsidence lasts only as long as the control of breath and vital forces continues; and when they are released, the mind also gets released and immediately, becoming externalized, it continues to wander through the force of its subtle tendencies.

The source of the mind is the same as that of breath and vital forces. It is really the multitude of thoughts that constitutes the mind; and the 'I'-thought is the primal thought of the mind, and is itself the ego. But breath too has its origin at the same place whence the ego rises. Therefore, when the mind subsides, breath and vital forces also subside; and conversely, when the latter subside, the former also subsides.

Breath and vital forces are also described as the gross manifestation of the mind. Till the hour of death the mind sustains and supports these forces in the physical body; and when life becomes extinct, the mind envelopes them and carries them away. During sleep, however, the vital forces continue to function, although the mind is not manifest. This is according to the divine law and is intended to protect the body and to remove any possible doubt as to whether it is dead or alive while one is asleep. Without such arrangement by nature, sleeping bodies would often be cremated alive. The vitality apparent in breathing is left behind by the mind as a 'watchman'. But in the wakeful state and in *samadhi*, when the mind subsides, breath also subsides. For this reason (because the mind has the sustaining and controlling power over breath and vital forces and is therefore ulterior to both of them), the practice of breath-control is merely helpful in subduing the mind but cannot bring about its final extinction.

Like breath-control, meditation on form, incantations, invocations and regulation of diet are only aids to control of the mind. Through the practice of meditation or invocation, the mind becomes one-pointed. Just as the elephant's trunk which is otherwise restless, will become steady if it is made to hold an iron chain, so that the elephant goes its way without reaching out for any other object, so also the ever-restless mind, which is trained and accustomed to a name or form through meditation or invocation, will steadily hold on to that alone.

When the mind is split up and dissipated into countless varying thoughts, each individual thought becomes extremely weak and inefficient. When, on the contrary, such thoughts subside more and more till they finally get destroyed, the mind becomes one-pointed and, thereby acquiring strength and power of endurance, easily reaches perfection in the method of enquiry in quest of the Self.

Regulation of diet, restricting it to *sattvic* food[6], taken in moderate quantity, is of all the rules of conduct the best; and it is most conducive to the development of the *sattvic* qualities[7] of the mind. These, in their turn, assist one in the practice of *Atma vichara* or enquiry in quest of the Self.

Countless *vishaya-vasanas* (subtle tendencies of the mind in relation to objects of sense-gratification), coming one after the other in quick succession like the waves of the ocean, agitate the

---

[6] i.e., simple and nutritious food which sustains but does not stimulate the physical body.

[7] Purity of heart, self-restraint, evenness of temper, tenderness towards all beings, fortitude and freedom from desire, hatred and arrogance are the outstanding virtues of the *sattvic* mind.

mind. Nevertheless they too subside and finally get destroyed with progressive practice of *Atma dhyana* or meditation on the Self. Without giving room even to the thought which occurs in the form of doubt, whether it is possible to stay merely as the very Self, whether all the *vasanas* can be destroyed, one should firmly and unceasingly carry on meditation on the Self.

However sinful a person may be, if he would stop wailing inconsolably: 'Alas! I am a sinner, how shall I attain Liberation?' and, casting away even the thought that he is a sinner, if he would zealously carry on meditation on the Self, he would most assuredly get reformed.

So long as subtle tendencies continue to inhere in the mind, it is necessary to carry on the enquiry, 'Who am I?'

As and when thoughts occur, they should, one and all, be annihilated then and there, at the very place of their origin, by the method of enquiry in quest of the Self.

Not to desire anything extraneous to oneself constitutes *vairagya* (dispassion) or *nirasa* (desirelessness). Not to give up one's hold on the Self constitutes *jnana* (knowledge). But really *vairagya* and *jnana* are one and the same. Just as the pearl-diver, tying stones to his waist, dives down into the depths, and gets the pearl from the sea-bed, so every aspirant, pledged to *vairagya* can dive deep into himself and realize the precious Atman. If the earnest seeker would only cultivate the constant and deep contemplative 'remembrance' (*smrti*) of the true nature of the Self till he has realized it, that alone would suffice. Distracting thoughts are like the enemy in the fortress. As long as they are in possession of it, they will certainly sally forth. But if, as and when they come out, you put them to the sword the fortress will finally be captured.

God and the Guru are not really different; they are identical. He that has earned the Grace of the Guru shall undoubtedly be saved and never forsaken, just as the prey that has fallen into the tiger's jaws will never be allowed to escape. But the disciple, for his part, should unswervingly follow the path shown by the Master.

Firm and disciplined inherence in the Atman without giving the least scope for the rise of any thought other than the deep contemplative thought of the Self, constitutes self-surrender to the Supreme Lord. Let any amount of burden be laid on Him, He will bear it all. It is, in fact, the indefinable power of the Lord that ordains, sustains and controls everything that happens. Why then, should we worry, tormented by vexatious thoughts, saying: 'Shall we act this way? No, that way,' instead of meekly but happily submitting to that Power? Knowing that the train carries all the weight, why indeed should we, the passengers travelling in it, carry our small individual articles of luggage on our laps to our great discomfort, instead of putting them aside and sitting at perfect ease?

That which is Bliss is also the Self. Bliss and the Self are not distinct and separate but are one and the same. And *That* alone is real. In no single one of the countless objects of the mundane world is there anything that can be called happiness. It is through sheer ignorance and unwisdom that we fancy that happiness is obtained from them. On the contrary, when the mind is externalized, it suffers pain and anguish. The truth is that every time our desires get fulfilled, the mind, turning to its source, experiences only that happiness which is natural to the Self. Similarly, in deep sleep, in spiritual trance (*samadhi*), when fainting, when a desired object is obtained, or when evil befalls an object considered undesirable, the mind turns inwards and enjoys that Bliss of Atman. Thus wandering astray forsaking the Self, and returning to it again and again is the interminable and wearisome lot of the mind.

It is pleasant under the shade of a tree and scorching in the heat of the sun outside. A person toiling in the sun seeks the cool shade of the tree and is happy under it. After staying there for a while, he moves out again but, unable to bear the merciless heat of the sun, he again seeks the shade. In this way he keeps on moving from shade to sun and sun to shade.

It is an unwise person who acts thus, whereas the wise man never leaves the shade: in the same way the mind of the Enlightened Sage (*jnani*) never exists apart from Brahman, the Absolute. The mind of the ignorant on the other hand, entering into the phenomenal world, suffers pain and anguish; and then, turning for a short while towards Brahman, it experiences happiness. Such is the mind of the ignorant.

This phenomenal world, however, is nothing but thought. When the world recedes from one's view — that is when one is free from thought — the mind enjoys the Bliss of the Self. Conversely, when the world appears — that is when thought occurs — the mind experiences pain and anguish.

Not from any desire, resolve or effort on the part of the rising sun, but merely due to the presence of his rays, the lens emits heat, the lotus blossoms, water evaporates, and people attend to their various duties in life. In the proximity of the magnet the needle moves. Similarly the soul or *jiva*, subjected to the threefold activity of creation, preservation, and destruction which takes place merely due to the unique Presence of the Supreme Lord, performs acts in accordance with its karma,[8] and subsides to rest after such activity. But the Lord Himself has no resolve; no act or event touches even the fringe of His Being. This state of immaculate aloofness can be likened to that of the sun, which is untouched by the activities of life, or to that of the

---

[8] i.e., the fruits of past actions which are being worked out in the present life.

all-pervasive ether, which is not affected by the interaction of the complex qualities of the other four elements.

All scriptures without any exception proclaim that for attaining Salvation, the mind should be subdued; and once one knows that control of the mind is their final aim, it is futile to make an interminable study of them. What is required for such control is actual enquiry into oneself by self-interrogation, 'Who am I?' How can this enquiry in quest of the Self be made merely by means of a study of the scriptures?

One should realize the Self by the Eye of Wisdom. Does Rama need a mirror to recognize himself as Rama? That to which the 'I' refers is within the five sheaths,[9] whereas the scriptures are outside them. Therefore, it is futile to seek by means of the study of scriptures the Self that has to be realized by summarily rejecting even the five sheaths.

To enquire 'Who am I that am in bondage?' and to know one's real nature is alone Liberation. To keep the mind constantly turned within and to abide thus in the Self, is alone *Atma-vichara* (Self-enquiry), whereas *dhyana* (meditation) consists in fervent contemplation of the Self as *Sat-Chit-Ananda* (Being-Consciousness-Bliss). Indeed, at some time, one will have to forget everything that has been learnt.

Just as it is futile to examine the rubbish that has to be swept up only to be thrown away, so it is futile for him who seeks to know the Self to set to work enumerating the *tattvas*[10] that envelop the Self and examining them instead of casting them away. He should consider the phenomenal world with reference to himself as merely a dream.

---

[9] These are the physical, vital, and mental sheaths, and the sheaths of Knowledge-Experience and of Blissful-ignorance.

[10] *Tattvas* are the elements into which phenomenal existence — from the subtle mind to gross matter — is classified.

Except that the wakeful state is long and the dream state short, there is no difference between the two. All the activities of the dream state appear, for the time being, just as real as the activities of the wakeful state seem to be while awake. Only, during the dream state, the mind assumes another form or a different bodily sheath. For thoughts on the one hand and name and form on the other occur simultaneously during both the wakeful and dream states.

There are not two minds, one good and the other evil. It is only the *vasanas* or tendencies of the mind that are of two kinds, good and favourable, evil and unfavourable. When the mind is associated with the former it is called good; and when associated with the latter it is called evil. However evil-minded other people may appear to you, it is not proper to hate or depise them. Likes and dislikes, love and hatred are equally to be eschewed. It is also not proper to let the mind often rest on objects or affairs of mundane life. As far as possible one should not interfere in the affairs of others. Everything offered to others is really an offering to oneself; and if only this truth were realized, who is there that would refuse anything to others?

If the ego rises, all else will also rise; if it subsides, all else will also subside. The deeper the humility with which we conduct ourselves, the better it is for us. If only the mind is kept under control, what matters it where one may happen to be?

Self-Enquiry

Self-Enquiry

II
SELF-ENQUIRY

CHAPTER I

WHO AM I?

*In this chapter is given clearly the path of
enquiry into the Self, or 'Who Am I?'*

Is not the sense of 'I' natural to all beings, expressed in all
their feelings as 'I came', 'I went', 'I did', or 'I was'? On
questioning what this is, we find that the body is identified with
'I' because movements and similar functions pertain to the body.
Can the body then be this 'I-consciousness'? It was not there
before birth, it is composed of the five elements, it is absent[1] in
sleep, and it (eventually) becomes a corpse. No, it cannot be.
This sense of 'I', which arises in the body for the time being, is
otherwise called the ego, ignorance, illusion, impurity, or
individual self. The purpose of all the scriptures is this enquiry
(into the Self). It is declared in them that the annihilation of
the ego-sense is Liberation. How then can one remain
indifferent to this teaching? Can the body, which is insentient
as a piece of wood, shine and function as 'I'? No. Therefore, lay
aside this insentient body as though it were truly a corpse. Do

---

[1] i.e. from our awareness.

not even murmur 'I', but enquire keenly within what it is that now shines within the heart as 'I'. Underlying the unceasing flow of varied thoughts, there arises the continuous, unbroken awareness, silent and spontaneous, as 'I-I' in the Heart. If one catches hold of it and remains still, it will completely annihilate the sense of 'I' in the body, and will itself disappear as a fire of burning camphor. Sages and scriptures proclaim this to be Liberation.

The veil of ignorance can never completely hide the self. How can it? Even the ignorant do not fail to speak of the 'I'. It only hides the Reality, 'I-am-the-Self', or 'I-am-pure-Consciousness', and confounds the 'I' with the body.

The Self is self-effulgent. One need give it no mental picture, anyway. The thought that imagines it is itself bondage, because the Self is the Effulgence transcending darkness and light; one should not think of it with the mind. Such imagination will end in bondage, whereas the Self spontaneously shines as the Absolute. This enquiry into the Self in devotional meditation evolves into the state of absorption of the mind into the Self and leads to Liberation and unqualified Bliss. The great sages have declared that only by the help of this devotional enquiry into the Self can Liberation be attained. Because the ego in the form of the 'I-thought' is the root of the tree of illusion, its destruction fells illusion, even as a tree is felled by the cutting of its roots. This easy method of annihilating the ego is alone worthy to be called *bhakti* (devotion), *jnana* (knowledge), *yoga* (union), or *dhyana* (meditation).

In the 'I-am-the-body' consciousness, the three bodies[2] composed of the five sheaths[3] are contained. If that mode of

---

[2] i.e., the physical, subtle and causal — of the waking, dream and sleep states respectively.

[3] i.e. the gross, sensory, mental, intellectual and blissful.

consciousness is removed all else drops off of its own accord; all other bodies depend on it. There is no need to eliminate them separately because the scriptures declare that thought alone is bondage. It is their final injunction that the best method is to surrender the mind in the form of the 'I'-thought to Him (the Self), and, keeping quite still, not forget Him.

CHAPTER II

THE MIND

In this chapter are described briefly the nature of the mind, its states and location

According to the Hindu scriptures an entity known as the 'mind', is derived from the subtle essence of the food consumed; which flourishes as love, hatred, lust, anger, and so on; which is the totality of mentality, intellect, desire, and ego; which, although it has such diverse functions, bears the generic name 'mind', which is objectified as the insentient objects cognized by us; which, though itself insentient, appears to be sentient, being associated with Consciousness, just as a piece of red-hot iron appears to be fire; in which the principle of differentiation is inherent; which is transient and is possessed of parts capable of being moulded into any shape like lac, gold, or wax; which is the basis of all root-principles *(tattvas);* which is located in the Heart like sight in the eye and hearing in the ear; which gives its character to the individual self and which, on thinking of the object already associated with the consciousness reflected on the brain, assumes a thought-form; which is in contact with that object through the five senses operated by the brain, which appropriates such cognizance to itself with the feeling 'I am cognizant of such and such', enjoys the object and is finally satisfied.

To think whether a certain thing may be eaten is a thought-form of the mind. 'It is good. It is not good. It can be eaten. It cannot be eaten'; discriminating notions like these constitute the discriminative intellect. Because the mind alone constitutes the root-principle manifesting as the three entities of ego, God, and world, its absorption and dissolution in the Self is the final emancipation known as *kaivalya,* which is the same as Brahman.

The senses, being located externally as aids for the cognition of objects, are exterior; the mind, being internal, is the inner sense. 'Within, and without' are relative to the body; they have no significance in the Absolute. For the purpose of showing the whole objective world to be within, and not without, the scriptures have described the cosmos as being shaped like the lotus of the Heart. But that is not other than the Self. Just as the goldsmith's wax ball, although hiding minute specks of gold, still looks like a simple lump of wax, so too all the individuals merged in dark ignorance *(avidya),* or the universal veiling *(maya),* are only aware of nescience in their sleep. In deep sleep the physical and subtle bodies, though entering in the dark veiling, still lie merged in the Self. From ignorance sprang the ego — the subtle body. The mind must be transformed into the Self.

Mind is, in reality, only consciousness, because it is pure and transparent by nature: in that pure state, however, it cannot be called mind. The wrong identification of one thing with another[1] is the work of the contaminated mind. That is to say,

---

[1] i.e. The mistaken view that attributes the Reality of the Self to the material world as existing by itself independent of the conscious principle. This is due to the false identification of the Self with the physical body, as a result of which the ignorant person assumes that what is outside and independent of the physical body is also outside and independent of the conscious principle.

the pure, uncontaminated mind, being absolute Consciousness, on becoming oblivious of its primary nature, is overpowered by the quality of darkness *(tamas)* and manifests as the physical world. Similarly, over-powered by activity *(rajas),* it identifies itself with the body and, appearing in the manifested world as 'I', mistakes this ego for the reality. Thus, swayed by love and hatred, it performs good and bad actions, and is, as the result, caught up in the cycle of births and deaths. It is the experience of everyone that in deep sleep and in a faint he has no awareness of his own Self or of objectivity. Later the experience 'I woke up from sleep', 'I regained consciousness', is the distinctive knowledge born of the natural state. This distinctive knowledge is called *vijnana.* It shines not by itself but by always adhering either to the Self or the non-Self. When it inheres in the Self, it is called true Knowledge; it is awareness of the mental mode in the Self, or perpetual awareness; and when this distinctive knowledge combines with the non-Self, it is called ignorance. The state in which it inheres in the Self and shines as the Self is termed *aham spurana* or the pulsation of the Self. This is not something apart from the Self; it is a sign of the forthcoming realization of the Self. However this is not the state of Primal Being. The source in which this pulsation is revealed is called *prajnana* (Consciousness). It is this source that Vedanta proclaims as *prajnana ghana.* The *Vivekachudamani* of Sankaracharya describes this Eternal State as follows: 'In the sheath of intelligence shines eternally Atman, the self-effulgent witness of all. Making that thy Goal, which is quite different from the unreal, enjoy it by experience, through unbroken thought-current as thy own Self.'

The ever luminous Self is one and universal. Notwithstanding the individual's experience of the three states — waking, dream, and deep sleep — the Self remains pure and changeless. It is not

limited by the three bodies: physical, mental and causal; and it
transcends the triple relation of seer, sight and seen. The diagram
in this page will be found helpful in understanding the changeless
state of the Self, transcending the illusory manifestations referred
to above.

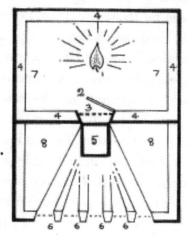

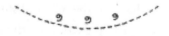

Diagram

1.	Flame	....	represents	the Self.
2.	Door	....	"	Sleep
3.	Doorway	....	"	Intellectual principle
		....		(mahat) as the source of
		....		the ego (ahankar).
4.	Inner wall	....	"	Ignorance (avidya).
5.	Crystal mirror	....	"	Ego
6.	Windows	....	"	Five Senses
7.	Inner chamber	....	"	Causal body during sleep
8.	Middle chamber	....	"	Subtle body in dream state
9.	Open court-yard	....	"	Physical body in waking state

    The inner and the middle chambers together with the open court-
yard represent the individual.

The sketch illustrates how the luminous Consciousness of the Self, shining by Itself, functions as the causal body (7) in the inner chamber surrounded by walls of ignorance *(avidya)* (4) and led by the door of sleep (2), which is moved by the vital forces, due to the lapse of time and according to destiny, through the doorway (3) against the interposed mirror of the ego (5). It passes with the light reflected therefrom into the middle chamber of the dream state (8); later is projected into the open courtyard of wakefulness (9) through the passage of the five senses or windows (6). When the door of sleep (2) is shut by the force of mind (i.e. the vital forces) due to the lapse of time and according to destiny, it retires from the wakeful and dream states into deep sleep and remains merely as itself without the ego-sense. The sketch also illustrates the serene existence of the Self as different from the ego and from the three states of sleep, dream and wakefulness.

The individual self resides in the eye during the waking state, in the neck[2] during the dream state, and in the Heart during deep sleep; but the Heart is the chief among these places, and therefore the individual self never entirely leaves the Heart. Although it is specifically said that the neck is the seat of the mind, the brain of the intellect, and the Heart or the whole body of the ego, still the scriptures state conclusively that the Heart is the seat of that totality of the inner senses[3] which is called the mind. The Sages, having investigated all the different versions of the scriptures, briefly stated the whole truth that it is the experience of everyone that the Heart is primarily the seat of the 'I'.

---

[2] At the back of the neck is the *medulla oblongata.*
[3] *Antahkarana,* in the original, meaning the mind, intellect and ego collectively.

CHAPTER III

THE WORLD

*In this chapter it is shown that the world has no reality
of its own and does not exist apart from the Self.*

Creation: The main purpose of the scriptures is to expose
the illusory nature of the world and to reveal the Supreme Spirit
as the only Reality. They have built up the theory of creation
with this sole end in view. They even go into details and
entertain the lowest order of seekers with the narration of the
successive appearance of the Spirit, of the disequilibrium[1] of
reflected consciousness, of the fundamentals of elements, of
the world, of the body, of life, and so on. But for the higher
order of seekers the scriptures would say, in short, that the whole
world appears like a panorama in a dream with an apparent
objectivity and independent existence due to ignorance of the
Self and consequent obsession with obtrusive thoughts. They
seek to show the world as an illusion in order to reveal the
Truth. Those who have realized the Self by direct and immediate
experience clearly perceive beyond all doubt that the
phenomenal world as an objective, independent reality is wholly
non-existent.

---

[1] *Prakrti,* in the oringinal meaning, the distrubance of the balance of
the three qualities in Nature, viz., harmony, activity, and darkness,
which precede the manifestation of primordial matter.

DISCRIMINATION BETWEEN THE SEER
AND THE SEEN

Object seen : insentient	*The seer : sentient*
The body, a pot, etc.	the eye
The eye	the optic nerve-centre in the brain
The optic nerve-centre	the mind
The mind	the individual self or ego
The individual self	pure Consciousness

Since the Self, which is pure Consciousness, cognizes everything, as stated in the classification above, it is the ultimate Seer. All the rest: ego, mind, etc., are merely its objects. The subject in one line becomes the object in the next; so each one of them except the Self or pure Consciousness is a merely externalized object and cannot be the true Seer. Since the Self cannot be objectified, not being cognized by anything else, and since the Self is the Seer seeing all else, the subject-object relation and the apparent subjectivity of the Self exist only on the plane of relativity and vanish in the Absolute. There is in truth no other than the Self, which is neither the seer nor the seen, and is not involved as subject or object.

CHAPTER IV

THE EGO (*JIVA*)

In this chapter the Self (Atma) *itself is said to be the ego* (Jiva) *and the nature of the ego is explained.*

The mind is nothing else than the 'I'-thought. The mind and the ego are one and the same. Intellect, will, ego, and individuality are collectively the same mind. It is like a man being variously described according to his different activities. The individual is nothing else than the ego which, again is only the mind. Simultaneously with the rise of the ego the mind appears, associated with the reflected nature of the Self, like the red-hot iron in the example.[1] How is the fire in the red-hot iron to be understood? As being one with it. Since the individual is nothing else than the ego and is inseparable from the Self, as the fire and the red-hot iron are, there is no other self to act as witness of the individual than the individual himself functioning as the ego, which after all is only the mind associated with reflected Consciousness. The very same Self not only shines unaffected in the Heart, like the fire in the iron,[2] but is also infinite like space. It is self-luminous in the Heart as pure Consciousness, as the One without a second and, manifesting universally as the same in all individuals, it is known as the Supreme Spirit. 'Heart' is merely another name for the Supreme Spirit, because He is in all Hearts.

Thus the red-hot iron is the individual, the fiery heat is the witnessing Self, the iron is the ego. The Pure fire is the all-immanent and all-knowing Supreme Spirit.

---

[1] It is a commonly used example in India that, just as red-hot iron partakes of the nature of fire through contact with it, so the mind or ego, partakes of the nature of Consciousness through contact with the Self.

[2] Just as the fire in the red-hot iron is unaffected by the hammer-blows, which only change the shape of the metal, so the vicissitudes of life, pleasure and pain, affect only the ego, the Self ever remaining pure and undefiled.

Chapter V

THE SUPREME BEING

In this chapter it is shown that the form of the Self is the form of God and He is in the form of 'I-I'

The universal principle underlying the correspondence between the ideas 'within' and the objects 'without' is the true significance of the term 'mind'. Therefore, the body and the world which appear as external to oneself are only mental reflections. It is only the Heart that manifests in all these forms. In the Core of the all-comprehensive Heart, that is, in the expanse of the pure mind, there is the self-luminous 'I' always shining. Because It is manifest in everybody, it is also called the Omniscient Witness, or the Fourth State.[1]

The Infinite Expanse is the Reality known as the Supreme Spirit or the Self, which shines without egoism as the Consciousness within the 'I', as the One in all individuals. What is beyond the Fourth State is only this. Let it be meditated on, the Expanse of Absolute Consciousness which shines, all-pervading, within and without, the illumination of the Fourth State, like space which simultaneously pervades the inmost blue core of a luminous flame and the innate space beyond. The true State is that which shines all over, as space includes and extends beyond the flame. No heed should be paid to the light. Enough to know that the Real is the State free from ego. That everyone points to the chest when referring to himself by gesture,

---

[1] Waking is the first state, dreaming is the second, and deep sleep is the third. Since pure Consciousness subsists during all the three states and also transcends them, it cannot strictly be classified along with the other three states, though it is technically called the Fourth State.

is sufficient proof that the Absolute resides as the Self in the Heart. The Rishi Vasishtha also says that searching for the Self outside oneself, oblivious of its constantly shining as 'I-I' within the Heart, is like throwing away an invaluable celestial gem for a sparkling pebble. Vedantists[2] consider it a sacrilege to regard the One Creating, Sustaining, and Absorbing Supreme Self as the separate gods, Ganapathi, Brahma, Vishnu, Rudra, Maheswara, and Sadasiva.[3]

Chapter VI

KNOWLEDGE OF THE SUPREME SELF

In this chapter is described the method of realizing the Self.

When the mind in the form of the ego, which takes the body for the Self and strays outwards, is curbed within the Heart the sense of 'I' in the body relinquished, and enquiry made with a still mind as to who it is that dwells in the body, a subtle illumination will be experienced as 'I-I' which is no other than the Absolute, the Self, seated in the lotus of the Heart, in the city of the body, the tabernacle of God. Then one should remain still, with the conviction that the Self shines as everything yet nothing, within, without, and everywhere, and is also the

---

[2] The adherents of the Hindu doctrine which postulates One Supreme Reality and dismisses the names and forms of all else as illusion.

[3] Ganapati is the son of Rudra, Brahma is the God of Creation, Vishnu of Preservation, Rudra or Siva of Destruction, Maheswara of universal veiling, Sadasiva is the Deity whose bestowal of Grace removes the veiling.

transcendental Being. This is known as meditation on the Truth conveyed by the dictum '*Sivoham*', 'I am Siva' and is also called the Fourth State.

That which is even beyond this subtle experience is God, variously termed the State beyond the Fourth, the Omnipresent, Supreme Being which shines as the Core of the Divine Flame within, and described as manifesting in concentration and meditation, the Sixth and Seventh steps of the Eightfold Yoga, the Expanse of the Heart, pure Consciousness, the Absolute shining in the mind's sky, Bliss, the Self, and Wisdom. By long, continuous, and steady practice of this meditation on the Self as 'I am the Supreme', the veil of ignorance in the Heart and all the resultant obstructions will be removed, and perfect Wisdom will result. Knowing in this manner the Real indwelling in the cavity of the Heart, in the tabernacle of the body, is indeed realizing the Absolute, which is inherent in all, because the Heart comprises all that exists. This is confirmed by the scriptural text, 'The Sage abides blissful in the city of nine gates which is the body', and 'The body is the temple, the individual self is the Absolute. If He is worshipped as "The Supreme I am", Liberation will result; the Spirit which bears the body in the form of five sheaths is the cavity; the cavity is only the Heart, the transcendental Being residing therein is the Lord of the Cave.' This method of realizing the Absolute is known as *dahara vidya* or Intuitive Knowledge of the Heart. What more is there to say? One should realize It by direct, immediate experience.

CHAPTER VII

WORSHIP OF GOD

*In this chapter it is said that perennial awareness of the
Self is real worship and penance* (tapas).

The purpose of worshipping the Impersonal Supreme
Being is the incessant remembrance of the truth that you are
Brahman, because the meditation 'I am Brahman' comprises
sacrifice, gifts, penance, ritual, prayer, yoga and worship. The
only way to overcome obstructions to your meditation is to
forbid the mind to dwell on them and to introvert it into the
Self and there witness unconcernedly all that happens; there is
no other method. Do not even for a moment lose sight of the
Self. Fixing the mind on the Self or the 'I' abiding in the Heart
is the perfection of yoga, meditation, wisdom, devotion and
worship. Since the Supreme Being abides as the Self, constant
surrender of the mind by absorption in the Self is said to
comprise all forms of worship. Mind controlled, all else is
controlled. The mind is itself the life-current; the ignorant say
that in form it looks like a coiled serpent.[1] The six subtle centres[2]
(chakras) are merely mental pictures and are meant for beginners
in yoga. We project ourselves into the idols and worship them,
because we do not understand true inward worship. Knowledge
of the Self, which knows all, is Knowledge in perfection.

[1] *Kundalini,* in the original, usually meaning a mysterious dynamic
force dormant at the base of the spine, whose arousal is said
to confer first thaumaturgic powers and then spiritual Illumination.
[2] These are said to be centres in the subtle body along the spine
from the sacral region to the top of the head: the life-currnet in its
upward passage forces its way into them and in doing so confers
thaumaturgic and other powers.

Distracted as we are by various thoughts, if we would continuously contemplate the Self, which is Itself God, this single thought would in due course replace all distraction and would itself ultimately vanish; the pure Consciousness that alone finally remains is God. This is Liberation. Never to be heedless of one's own all-perfect, pure Self is the acme of yoga, wisdom, and all other forms of spiritual practice. Even though the mind wanders restlessly, involved in external matters, and so is forgetful of its own Self, one should remain alert and remember: 'The body is not I. Who am I?' Enquire in this way, turning the mind backward to its primal state. The enquiry 'Who am I?' is the only method of putting an end to all misery and ushering in supreme Beatitude. Whatever may be said and however phrased, this is the whole truth in a nutshell.

CHAPTER VIII

LIBERATION

This chapter teaches that Liberation can indeed be obtained by constant and prolonged meditation on the Self in the form of 'Sivoham' (I am Siva) which means 'I am Atman'. The characteristics of Jivanmukti (Liberation in this life) and Videhamukti (Liberation after death) are described.

Because the individual self, which is nothing but the mind, has lost the knowledge of its identity with the real Self, and has enmeshed itself in bondage, its search for the Self, its own eternal primal nature, resembles that of the shepherd searching for a lamb which all the time he bears on his own shoulders.

However, the Self-oblivious ego, even when once made aware of the Self, does not get Liberation, that is Self-Realization, on account of the obstruction of accumulated mental tendencies. It frequently confuses the body with the Self, forgetting that it is itself in truth the Self. Long-cultivated tendencies can indeed be eradicated by long-continued meditation: 'I am not the body, the senses, the mind, etc., I am the Self'. Therefore, the ego, that is the mind, which is nothing but a bundle of tendencies, and which confuses the body with 'I', should be subdued, and thus should the supreme liberated State known as Self-Realization be reached after prolonged devotional worship of the divine Self, which is the very Being of all the gods. This self-investigation annihilates the mind, and itself gets destroyed eventually, just as a stick used to stir the funeral pyre is itself finally burnt. This is the state of Liberation.

Self, Wisdom, Knowledge, Consciousness, the Absolute and God denote the same thing.

Can a man become a high officer by merely once seeing such an officer? He may become one if he strives and equips himself for the position. Similarly, can the ego, which is in bondage as the mind, become the divine Self, simply because it has once glimpsed that it is the Self? Is this not impossible without the destruction of the mind? Can a beggar become a king by merely visiting a king and declaring himself one? Similarly, unless the bond of the mind is cut asunder by prolonged and unbroken meditation, 'I am the Self, the Absolute', it is impossible to attain the transcendental State of Bliss, which is identical with the annihilation of the mind. 'The Self is the Absolute and the Absolute is the Self. The Self is the Absolute alone. That which is covered with husk is paddy, and when de-husked becomes rice. So also, when under bondage of action one is the individual self, and when the veil is removed one shines as the Absolute'. Thus proclaim the scriptures, which further declare: 'The mind should be drawn within and restrained in the Heart until the ego-sense, which sprouts as the ignorant mind, is therein destroyed. This is wisdom and meditation as well; all else is mere lecturing and pedantry', and, in consonance with this final word, one should fix the mind on Him, be aware of Him and realize Him by every possible endeavour.

Just as a Brahmin actor does not forget that he is a Brahmin, whatever part he may be acting, so also a man should not confuse himself with his body, but should have a firm awareness of his being the Self, whatever his activity may be. This awareness will manifest as the mind gets absorbed in its own primal State. Such absorption leads to Bliss Supreme, when the Self reveals itself spontaneously. Then one will not be affected by pleasure and pain, which result from contact with external objects. Everything will be perceived without attachment, as in a dream. Such thoughts as 'Is this good or that?' 'Is this to be done or that?' should not be allowed to arise. Immediately a thought arises, it should be annihilated at its source. If entertained even for a little while, it will hurl one down headlong like a treacherous friend. Can the mind which is fixed in its original State possess an ego-sense or have any problem to solve? Do not such thoughts themselves constitute bondage? Hence when such thoughts arise due to past tendencies, not only should the mind be curbed and turned back to its true State but also it should be made to remain unconcerned and indifferent to external happenings. Is it not due to Self-forgetfulness that such thoughts arise and cause more and more misery? Though the discriminating thought, 'I am not the doer; all actions are merely the reactions of the body, senses and mind,' is an aid for turning the mind back to its primal state, nevertheless it is still a thought, but one which is necessary for those minds which are addicted to much thinking. On the other hand, can the mind, fixed unswervingly in the divine Self and remaining unaffected even while engaged in activities, give in to such thoughts as 'I am the body. I am engaged in work', or again to the discriminating thought, 'I am not the doer, these actions are merely reactions of the body, senses and mind'? Gradually one should, by all possible means, try always to be aware of the Self. Everything is achieved if one succeeds in this. Let not the mind be diverted to any other object. One should abide in the Self without the sense of being the doer, even when engaged in work born of destiny, like a madman. Have not many devotees achieved much with a detached attitude and firm devotion of this nature?

Because the quality of purity *(sattva)* is the real nature of the mind, clearness like that of the unclouded sky is the characteristic of the mind-expanse. Being stirred up by the quality of activity *(rajas)* the mind becomes restless and, influenced by darkness *(tamas),* manifests as the physical world. The mind thus becoming restless on the one hand and appearing as solid matter on the other, the Real is not discerned. Just as fine silk threads cannot be woven with the use of a heavy iron shuttle, or the delicate shades of a work of art be distinguished in the light of a lamp flickering in the wind, so is Realization of Truth impossible with the mind rendered gross by darkness *(tamas)* and restless by activity *(rajas),* because Truth is exceedingly subtle and serene. Mind will be cleared of its impurities only by a desireless performance of duties during several births, getting a worthy Master, learning from him and incessantly practising meditation on the Supreme. The transformation of the mind into the world of inert matter due to the quality of darkness *(tamas)* and its restlessness due to the quality of activity *(rajas)* will cease. Then the mind regains its subtlety and composure. The Bliss of the Self can manifest only in a mind rendered subtle and steady by assiduous meditation. He who experiences that Bliss is liberated even while still alive.

When the mind is divested of the qualities of darkness and activity by constant meditation, the Bliss of the Self will clearly manifest within the subtle mind. Yogis gain omniscience by means of such mind-expanse. He alone who has achieved such subtlety of mind and has gained Realization of the Self is Liberated while still alive. The same state has been described in *Rama Gita*[1] as the Brahman beyond attributes, the one universal undifferentiated Spirit. He who has attained the unbroken eternal State beyond even that, transcending mind and speech, is called *videhamukta;* that is, when even the aforesaid subtle mind is destroyed, the experience of Bliss as such also ceases. He is drowned and dissolved in the fathomless Ocean of Bliss and is unaware of anything apart. This is *videhamukti.* There is nothing beyond it. It is the end of all.

As one continues to abide as the Self, the experience 'I am the Supreme Spirit' grows and becomes natural: the restlessness of the mind and the thought of the world in due course become extinct. Because experience is not possible without the mind, Realization takes place with the subtle mind. Since *videhamukti* connotes the entire dissolution of even the subtle mind, this State is beyond experience. It is the transcendental State. 'I am not the body. I am the pure Spirit' is the clear and indubitable experience of the *jivanmukta,* that is one who is liberated while yet alive. Nevertheless, if the mind is not totally destroyed, there is the possibility of his becoming apparently unhappy in his incidental association with objects, as ordained by his destiny. He may also appear to the onlooker as not having realized the unbroken eternal Bliss, because his mind seems to be agitated. However, the Bliss of Liberation in life is possible only to the mind made subtle and serene by long continued meditation.

---

[1] Ancient Hindu sacred work.

Chapter IX

THE EIGHTFOLD PATH OF YOGA

*In this chapter is described the path of yoga for
obtaining Self-Realization, getting control of the
mind through control of breath.*

For achieving devotion in the form of meditation described
in the previous chapter, steps like *yama* and *niyama* (the first
two stages in *ashtanga* or eightfold yoga, explained below) are
prescribed. These have two forms, one of the nature of yoga
and the other of *jnana*. Control over breath is yoga. Elimination
of the mind is *jnana*. Which of these comes more easily to the
aspirant depends on his inherent tendencies and maturity. Both
lead to the same result since by control of breath the mind gets
controlled, and by elimination of the mind the breath gets
controlled. The object of both these methods is the subsidence
and elimination of the mind.

Yama (moral self-control which is necessary preliminary
to the yogic path; in detail: abstention from lying, killing, theft,
lust and covetousness), *niyama* (disciplinary observances), *asana*
(postures), *pranayama* (breath-control), *pratyahara* (withdrawal
of the senses from external objects), *dharana* (concentrated
attention), *dhyana* (steady uninterrupted contemplation) and
samadhi (identification of oneself with the Atman). These eight
are the elements of yoga. Of these breath-control consists of
exhalation, inhalation and retention. While in all the *sastras* it
is said that exhalation and inhalation should be equal and
retention twice their length, in Rajayoga, retention of breath is
four times as long as inhalation and twice as long as exhalation.
The breath-control of the Rajayoga path is superior to other

kinds. If this breath-control is practised according to one's capacity, without strain but regularly, the body gets fatigued in a way but becomes still and the desire to be in a state of Bliss gradually arises in the mind. Then *pratyahara* must be attempted. This unifies the mind and makes it one-pointed, so that it does not run after the external objects of name and form. Since the mind that has till now run after externals can rarely withdraw and steady itself, efforts are made to unify and steady it by holding it to a particular aim by the following means: *pranava japa* (the incantation of OM) and other incantations made mentally; fixing the attention between the eyebrows; concentrating on the tip of the nose; hearing the sounds arising within the ears alternately, i.e., striving to hear the sound in the left ear with the right ear and *vice versa*. *Dharana* (concentrated attention) must then be attempted. This means fixing the mind on a centre fit for meditation. The heart and *brahmarandhra* (fontanelle of aperture in the crown of the head) are recommended as fit spots for *dharana*. The mind is fixed on either of these spots while conceiving of one's personal deity in the form of a flame of light shining there. If one fixes one's attention on the heart it is the eight-petalled lotus; if on the *brahmarandhra* it is also the eight-petalled lotus, though said to consist of *sahasradala* (a thousand petals) or 125 small petals.

Thus concentrating, one must meditate that one is not a separate being from one's deity and that that flame of light is the form of one's Atma (Spirit or Self). In other words, it is meditation on 'I am He'. The scripture says that the all-pervasive Brahman itself is shining in the heart as 'I-I', the witness of the intellect. If one asks 'Who am I?' then He (the Deity or the Atma) will be found shining (throbbing) as 'I-I', in the lotus of the heart. Practising this is also meditation and is much better than the 'I am He' meditation. A man can practise whatever comes easy to him. By practice of this kind of meditation, one becomes unaware of oneself and what one is doing and one's mind gets absorbed in the Self. The subtle state in which even the pulsation subsides is the state of *samadhi*. Only, one must guard against sleep in this state. Then it will confer Supreme Bliss. If anyone practises this daily and regularly, God will bless him on the Supreme Path, on which he will attain perfect Peace. As there are elaborate treatises on the elements of *ashtanga* yoga, only as much as is necessary is written here. Anyone who desires to know more must resort to a practising yogi with experience and learn from him in detail.

Pranava is incantation of OM with three and a half units, A, U, M, and a half unit of M. Of these A stands for the waking state, the gross body and creation, U stands for the dream state, the subtle body and preservation, M stands for deep sleep, the self at rest in sleep, the causal body and dissolution. The half unit stands for the fourth state, the true state of the I or Self. The state beyond this is the state of pure Bliss. The fourth state obtained in meditation as one's true State contains within itself A, U, M and the half unit and so is called the state in which all sound forms have subsided; it is also called silent incantation and non-dual incantation, which is the essence of all incantations. It is for obtaining this true experience of OM that in the stage of *pratyahara*, silent incantation, is prescribed.

'The soul attains conscious immortality through meditating upon that principle ever shining like the flame of light possessing the effulgence of lightning, residing as All-Pervading in the midst of the heart lotus with eight-petals, the size of a thumb and described variously as *kailasa*, *vaikunta*, and *paramapada*'. The seeker is advised to meditate in accordance with this text. A sense of inconstancy in the Self may appear to arise and also of differentiation between the meditator and what he meditates upon. The seeker is advised to meditate upon his own Self because that flame which is throbbing as I-I is the Self. Therefore there need be no doubting this scriptural text. Of all forms of meditation *atma dhyana* (meditation on the Self), which has just been described, is the best. If that is achieved there is no need to attempt other forms of meditation, because all are included in it. Other forms are advised only to help achieve success in this. The form of meditation one follows will depend on one's maturity of mind. Though the various modes of meditation may appear different, yet they all converge on the same point; there is no need to doubt this. 'Knowing one's own Self is knowing God. Not knowing the nature of him who meditates but meditating on God as foreign to one's own Self is like measuring one's shadow with one's foot. You go on measuring while the shadow also goes on receding further and further.' So say the scriptures. Hence meditation on the Self is the best, because the Self alone is the Supreme Self of all the gods.

Chapter X

THE EIGHTFOLD PATH OF KNOWLEDGE

In this chapter is described the jnanamarga
(the path of Knowledge) which leads to Self-Realization
through realization that the Supreme is
One and Indivisible.

Detailed description of the phases of *jnana ashtanga* (the eightfold path of Knowledge) such as *yama* and *niyama* is beyond the scope of this small work. Exhalation in this path means giving up the two aspects of name and form, of body and world. Inhalation is taking in (grasping) the *sat* (being), *chit* (consciousness), *ananda* (bliss), aspects pervading names and forms. Retention of breath is retaining them, assimilating what has been taken in. *Pratyahara* is being ever on the vigil that the rejected names and forms do not intrude again into the mind. *Dharana* is retaining the mind in the heart, so that it does not wander, by holding firm to the concept already grasped, that is: 'I am the *sat-chit-ananda Atman*' (the Self which is Being-Consciousness-Bliss). *Dhyana* (meditation) is steady abidance as *aham swarupa* (in one's true form) which is experienced as 'I-I' of its own accord, just as when enquiring 'Who am I?', by stilling this corpse of a body of five sheaths. For this kind of breath-control there is no need of such regulations as *asanas* (postures) etc. One may practise it in any place or time. The primary aim is to fix the mind in the Heart at the feet of the Lord shining as the Self and never to forget Him. Forgetfulness of the Self is the source of all misery. Elders say that such forgetfulness is death to the aspirant after Liberation. It may be asked if the regular breath-control of Rajayoga (a yogic path) is unnecessary. To this we reply: it is useful, but its value lasts only as long as one is practising it, whereas the breath-control of the eightfold path of Knowledge is a permanent help. The aim of both kinds of breath-control is to remember the Self and to still the mind. Therefore until the mind has subsided in the heart by means of breath-control or Self-enquiry regular yogic breath-control remains necessary; further than that there is no need for it. The *kevala kumbhaka* type of breath-control is of such nature that the breathing subsides in the Heart even without control of inhalation and exhalation. One may practise the methods of either yoga or *jnana* (knowledge) as one chooses.

All the scriptures aim at control of the mind since destruction of the mind is *moksha* or Liberation. Yoga is control of the breath, while the methods of *jnana* or Knowledge is to see everything as a form of truth or as Brahman the One and Indivisible. It depends on a person's maturity which of these two paths will appeal to him. The path of knowledge is like taming an unruly bull by showing it a bundle of grass, that of yoga is like taming it by beating and yoking it. So say those who know. Fully competent persons reach the goal by controlling the mind established and fixed in the truth of Vedanta, knowing the certainty of the Self, and seeing their Self and everything as Brahman. Those who are less qualified fix the mind in the heart by means of breath-control and prolonged meditation on the Self. Those who are still less qualified reach higher stages by methods such as breath-control. Bearing this in mind, the yoga of the control of mind is classified as the eight-fold path of Knowledge and of yoga. It is enough if breath-control is practised till *kevala kumbhaka* is achieved.

Direct experience of *samadhi* can also be attained by devotion *(bhakti)* in the form of constant meditation *(dhyana)*. *Kevala kumbhaka* with Self-enquiry, even without control of inhalation and exhalation, is an aid to this. If that becomes natural to one, it can be practised at all times even during worldly activity and there is no need to seek a special place for it. Whatever a person finds suitable may be practised. If the mind gradually subsides, it does not matter if other things come or go. In the *Bhagavad Gita*, Lord Krishna says that the devotee is higher than the yogi and that the means to Liberation is bhakti (devotion) in the form of continuous or prolonged meditation on the Self, which is the sole Reality. Therefore if, somehow or other, we get the strength to rest the mind perpetually in Him, why worry about other things?

Chapter XI

RENUNCIATION

In this chapter the entire effacement of thought is said to be the only true sannyasa *(renunciation).*

Sannyasa or renunciation is not the discarding of external things but of the ego. To such renouncers *(sannyasins)* there exists no difference between solitude and active life. The Rishi Vasistha says: 'Just as a man, whose mind is preoccupied, is not aware of what is in front of him, so also the Sage, though engaged in work, is not the doer thereof, because his mind is immersed in the Self without the uprising of the ego. Just as a man lying on his bed dreams that he is falling headlong over a precipice, so also the ignorant person whose ego is still present, though engaged in deep meditation in solitude, does not cease to be the doer of all action.'

Chapter XII

CONCLUSION

It is within our power to adopt a simple and nutritious diet and, with earnest and incessant endeavour, to eradicate the ego — the cause of all misery — by stopping all mental activity born of the ego.

Can obsessing thoughts arise without the ego, or can there be illusion apart from such thoughts?

Therefore meditate incessantly upon the Self and obtain the Supreme Bliss of Liberation. This indeed is the purport of this work.

———

Spiritual
Instruction

III
Spiritual Instruction
(Upadesa Manjari)

Invocation

I seek refuge at the sacred feet of the blessed Ramana, who performs the entire work of creation, preservation and destruction, while remaining wholly unattached, and who makes us aware of what is real and thus protects us, that I may set down his words fittingly.

Importance of the Work

Worshipping with the instruments (of thought, word and body) the sacred lotus feet of Bhagavan Sri Ramana Maharshi, the very embodiment of the beginningless infinite supreme Brahman, the *Satchitananda* (existence, consciousness, bliss), I have gathered this bouquet of the flowers of his instructions (*upadesa manjari*) for the benefit of those who are foremost among the seekers of liberation and who are adored by learned persons, in order that they might adorn themselves with it and attain salvation.

This book is an epitome of the immortal words of that great soul, Sri Ramana Maharshi, whose teachings entirely dispelled the doubts and wrong notions of this humble person even as the sun dispels darkness.

The subject of this book is that eternal Brahman which shines as the pinnacle and heart of all the Vedas and Agamas.

That incomparable Self-realization (*atmasiddhi*) which is praised by all the Upanishads and which is the supreme good to be sought by all noble aspirants (*brahmavids*) is the theme of this work.

* * *

Chapter I

INSTRUCTION
(*Upadesa*)

1. *What are the marks of a real teacher* (Sadguru)?

Steady abidance in the Self, looking at all with an equal eye, unshakeable courage at all times, in all places and circumstances, etc.

2. *What are the marks of an earnest disciple* (sadsishya)?

An intense longing for the removal of sorrow and attainment of joy and an intense aversion for all kinds of mundane pleasure.

3. *What are the characteristics of instruction* (upadesa)?

The word '*upadesa*' means, 'near the place or seat' (*upa* - near, *desa* - place or seat). The Guru who is the embodiment of that which is indicated by the terms *sat, chit,* and *ananda* (existence, consciousness and bliss), prevents the disciple who, on account of his acceptance of the forms of the objects of the senses, has swerved from his true state and is consequently distressed and buffeted by joys and sorrows, from continuing so and establishes him in his own real nature without differentiation.

Upadesa also means showing a distant object quite near. It is brought home to the disciple that *Brahman* which he believes to be distant and different from himself is near and not different from himself.

4. *If it be true that the Guru is one's own Self* (atman), *what is the principle underlying the doctrine which says that, however learned a disciple may be or whatever occult powers he may possess, he cannot attain Self-realization* (atmasiddhi) *without the grace of the Guru?*

Although in absolute truth the state of the Guru is that of oneself it is very hard for the Self which has become the individual soul (*jiva*) through ignorance to realize its true state or nature without the grace of the Guru.

All mental concepts are controlled by the mere presence of the real Guru. If he were to say to one who arrogantly claims that he has seen the farther shore of the ocean of learning or one who claims arrogantly that he can perform deeds which are well-nigh impossible, "Yes, you learnt all that is to be learnt, but have you learnt (to know) yourself? And you who are capable of performing deeds which are almost impossible, have you seen yourself?", they will bow their heads (in shame) and remain silent. Thus it is evident that only by the grace of the Guru and by no other accomplishment is it possible to know oneself.

5. *What are the marks of the Guru's grace?*
   It is beyond words or thoughts.
6. *If that is so, how is it that it is said that the disciple realizes his true state by the Guru's grace?*
   It is like the elephant which wakes up on seeing a lion in its dream. Even as the elephant wakes up at the mere sight of the lion, so too is it certain that the disciple wakes up from the

sleep of ignorance into the wakefulness of true knowledge through the Guru's benevolent look of grace.

7. *What is the significance of the saying that the nature of the real Guru is that of the Supreme Lord* (Sarveshwara)?

In the case of the individual soul which desires to attain the state of true knowledge or the state of Godhood (*Ishwara*) and with that object always practises devotion, the Lord who is the witness of that individual soul and identical with it, comes forth, when the individual's devotion has reached a mature stage, in human form with the help of *sat-chit-ananda*. His three natural features, and form and name which he also graciously assumes, and in the guise of blessing the disciple, absorbs him in Himself. According to this doctrine the Guru can truly be called the Lord.

8. *How then did some great persons attain knowledge without a Guru?*

To a few mature persons the Lord shines as the light of knowledge and imparts awareness of the truth.

9. *What is the end of devotion* (bhakti) *and the path of* Siddhanta *(i.e.,* Saiva Siddhanta)?

It is to learn the truth that all one's actions performed with unselfish devotion, with the aid of the three purified instruments (body, speech and mind), in the capacity of the servant of the Lord, become the Lord's actions, and to stand forth free from the sense of 'I' and 'mine'. This is also the truth of what the *Saiva Siddhantins* call *parabhakti* (supreme devotion) or living in the service of God *(irai-pani-nittral)*.

10. *What is the end of the path of knowledge* (jnana) *or* Vedanta?

It is to know the truth that the 'I' is not different from the Lord (*Ishwara*) and to be free from the feeling of being the doer *(kartritva, ahamkara)*.

11. *How can it be said that the end of both these paths is the same?*

Whatever the means, the destruction of the sense of 'I' and 'mine' is the goal, and as these are interdependent, the destruction of either of them causes the destruction of the other; therefore in order to achieve that state of silence which is beyond thought and word, either the path of knowledge which removes the sense of 'I' or the path of devotion which removes the sense of 'mine', will suffice. So there is no doubt that the end of the paths of devotion and knowledge is one and the same.

Note: So long as the 'I' exists it is necessary to accept the Lord also. If any one wishes to regain easily the supreme state of identity (sayujya) *now lost to him, it is only proper that he should accept this conclusion.*

12. *What is the mark of the ego?*

The individual soul of the form of 'I' is the ego. The Self which is of the nature of intelligence (*chit*) has no sense of 'I'. Nor does the insentient body possess a sense of 'I'. The mysterious appearance of a delusive ego between the intelligent and the insentient being the root cause of all these troubles, upon its destruction by whatever means, that which really exists will be seen as it is. This is called liberation (*moksha*).

CHAPTER II

PRACTICE
(*Abhyasa*)

1.   *What is the method of practice?*

As the Self of a person who tries to attain Self-realization is not different from him and as there is nothing other than or superior to him to be attained by him, Self-realization being only the realization of one's own nature, the seeker of liberation realizes, without doubts or misconceptions, his real nature by distinguishing the eternal from the transient, and never swerves from his natural state. This is known as the practice of knowledge. This is the enquiry leading to Self-realization.

2.   *Can this path of enquiry be followed by all aspirants?*

This is suitable only for ripe souls. The rest should follow different methods according to the state of their minds.

3.   *What are the other methods?*

They are (i) *stuti*, (ii) *japa*, (iii) *dhyana*, (iv) yoga, (v) *jnana*, etc.

(i) *Stuti* is singing the praises of the Lord with a great feeling of devotion.

(ii) *Japa* is uttering the names of the gods or sacred *mantras* like *Om* either mentally or verbally. (While following the methods of *stuti* and *japa* the mind will sometimes be concentrated (*lit.* closed) and sometimes diffused (*lit.* open). The vagaries of the mind will not be evident to those who follow these methods).

(iii) *Dhyana* denotes the repetition of the names, etc., mentally (*japa*) with feelings of devotion. In this method the state of the mind will be understood easily. For the mind does not become concentrated and diffused simultaneously. When one is in *dhyana* it does not contact the objects of the senses, and when it is in contact with the objects it is not in *dhyana*. Therefore those who are in this state can observe the vagaries of the mind then and there and by stopping the mind from thinking other thoughts, fix it in *dhyana*. Perfection in *dhyana* is the state of abiding in the Self (*lit.*, abiding in the form of 'That' — *tadakaranilai*).

As meditation functions in an exceedingly subtle manner at the source of the mind it is not difficult to perceive its rise and subsidence.

(iv) Yoga: The source of the breath is the same as that of the mind; therefore the subsidence of either leads effortlessly to that of the other. The practice of stilling the mind through breath control (*pranayama*) is called yoga.

Fixing their minds on psychic centres such as the *sahasrara* (*lit.* the thousand-petalled lotus) *yogis* remain for any length of time without awareness of their bodies. As long as this state continues they appear to be immersed in some kind of joy. But when the mind which has become tranquil emerges (becomes active again) it resumes its worldly thoughts. It is therefore necessary to train it with the help of practices like *dhyana*, whenever it becomes externalised. It will then attain a state in which there is neither subsidence nor emergence.

(v) *Jnana* is the annihilation of the mind in which it is made to assume the form of the Self through the constant practice of *dhyana* or enquiry (*vichara*). The extinction of the mind is the state in which there is a cessation of all efforts. Those who are established in this state never swerve from their true state. The terms 'silence' (*mauna*) and inaction refer to this state alone.

Note: (1) All practices are followed only with the object of concentrating the mind. As all the mental activities like remembering, forgetting, desiring, hating, attracting, discarding, etc., are modifications of the mind, they cannot be one's true state. Simple, changeless being is one's true nature. Therefore to know the truth of one's being and to be it, is known as release from bondage and the destruction of the knot (granthi nasam). *Until this state of tranquillity of mind is firmly attained, the practice of unswerving abidance in the Self and keeping the mind unsoiled by various thoughts is essential for an aspirant.*

(2) Although the practices for achieving strength of mind are numerous, all of them achieve the same end. For it can be seen that whoever concentrates his mind on any object, will, on the cessation of all mental concepts, ultimately remain merely as that object. This is called successful meditation (dhyana siddhi). *Those who follow the path of enquiry realize that the mind which remains at the end of the enquiry is* Brahman. *Those who practise meditation realize that the mind which remains at the end of the meditation is the object of their meditation. As the result is the same in either case it is the duty of aspirants to practise continuously either of these methods till the goal is reached.*

4.   *Is the state of 'being still' a state involving effort or effortless?*

It is not an effortless state of indolence. All mundane activities which are ordinarily called effort are performed with the aid of a portion of the mind and with frequent breaks. But the act of communion with the Self (*atma vyavahara*) or remaining still inwardly is intense activity which is performed with the entire mind and without break.

Maya (delusion or ignorance) which cannot be destroyed by any other act is completely destroyed by this intense activity which is called 'silence' (*mauna*).

5.   *What is the nature of* maya?

Maya is that which makes us regard as non-existent the Self, the Reality, which is always and everywhere present, all-pervasive and self-luminous, and as existent the individual soul (*jiva*), the world (*jagat*), and God (*para*) which have been conclusively proved to be non-existent at all times and places.

6. *As the Self shines fully of its own accord why is it not generally recognised like the other objects of the world by all persons?*

Wherever particular objects are known it is the Self which has known itself in the form of those objects. For what is known as knowledge or awareness is only the patency of the Self (*atma shakti*). The Self is the only sentient object. There is nothing apart from the Self. If there are such objects they are all insentient and therefore cannot either know themselves or mutually know one another. It is because the Self does not know its true nature in this manner that it seems to be immersed and struggling in the ocean of birth (and death) in the form of the individual soul.

7. *Although the Lord is all-pervasive it appears, from passages like 'adorning him through His grace', that He can be known only through His grace. How then can the individual soul by its own efforts attain Self-realization in the absence of the Lord's grace?*

As the Lord denotes the Self and as grace means the Lord's presence or revelation, there is no time when the Lord remains unknown. If the light of the sun is invisible to the owl it is only the fault of that bird and not of the sun. Similarly can the unawareness by ignorant persons of the Self which is always of the nature of awareness be other than their own fault? How can it be the fault of the Self? It is because grace is of the very nature of the Lord that He is well known as 'the blessed grace'. Therefore the Lord, whose nature itself is grace, does not have to bestow His grace. Nor is there any particular time for bestowing His grace.

8.   *What part of the body is the abode of the Self?*

The heart on the right side of the chest is generally indicated. This is because we usually point to the right side of the chest when we refer to ourselves. Some say that the *sahasrara* (the thousand-petalled lotus) is the abode of the Self. But if that were true the head should not fall forward when we go to sleep or faint.

9.   *What is the nature of the heart?*

The sacred texts describing it say:

Between the two breasts, below the chest and above the abdomen, there are six organs of different colours[1]. One of them resembling the bud of a water lily and situated two digits to the right is the heart. It is inverted and within it is a tiny orifice which is the seat of dense darkness (ignorance) full of desires. All the psychic nerves (*nadis*) depend upon it. It is the abode of the vital forces, the mind and the light (of consciousness).[2]

But, although it is described thus, the meaning of the word heart (*hridayam*) is the Self (*Atman*). As it is denoted by the terms existence, consciousness, bliss, eternal and plenum (*sat, chit, anandam, nityam, purnam*) it has no differences such as exterior and interior or up and down. That tranquil state in which all thoughts come to an end is called the state of the Self. When it is realized as it is, there is no scope for discussions about its location inside the body or outside.

10. *Why do thoughts of many objects arise in the mind even when*
     there is no contact with external objects?

All such thoughts are due to latent tendencies (*purva samskaras*). They appear only to the individual consciousness (*jiva*) which has forgotten its real nature and become

---

[1] These are not the same as the *chakras*.

[2] See *Reality in Forty Verses: Supplement*, 18-19.

externalised. Whenever particular things are perceived, the enquiry 'Who is it that sees them?' should be made; they will then disappear at once.

11. *How do the triple factors (i.e., knower, known and knowledge), which are absent in deep sleep, samadhi, etc., manifest themselves in the Self (in the states of waking and dreaming)?*

From the Self there arise in succession:

(i) *Chidabhasa* (reflected consciousness) which is a kind of luminosity.

(ii) *Jiva* (the individual consciousness) or the seer or the first concept.

(iii) Phenomena, that is the world.

12. *Since the Self is free from the notions of knowledge and ignorance how can it be said to pervade the entire body in the shape of sentience or to impart sentience to the senses?*

Wise men say that there is a connection between the source of the various psychic nerves and the Self, that this is the knot of the heart, that the connection between the sentient and the insentient will exist until this is cut asunder with the aid of true knowledge, that just as the subtle and invisible force of electricity travels through wires and does many wonderful things, so the force of the Self also travels through the psychic nerves and, pervading the entire body, imparts sentience to the senses, and that if this knot is cut, the Self will remain as it always is, without any attributes.

13. *How can there be a connection between the Self which is pure knowledge and the triple factors which are relative knowledge?*

This is, in a way, like the working of a cinema as shown in the next page.

Just as the pictures appear on the screen as long as the film throws the shadows through the lens, so the phenomenal world

CINEMA SHOW	SELF
(i) The lamp inside (the apparatus)	(i) The Self
(ii) The lens in front of the lamp.	(ii) The pure (*sattvic*) mind close to the Self.
(iii) The film which is a long series of (separate photos).	(iii) The stream of latent tendencies consisting of subtle thoughts.
(iv) The lens, the light passing through it and the lamp, which together form the focussed light.	(iv) The mind, the illumination of it and the Self, which together form the seer or the *Jiva*.
(v) The light passing through the lens and falling on the screen	(v) The light of the Self emerging from the mind through the senses, and falling on the world.
(vi) The various kinds of pictures appearing in the light of the screen.	(vi) The various forms and names appearing as the objects perceived in the light of the world.
(vii) The mechanism which sets the film in motion.	(vii) The divine law manifesting the latent tendencies of the mind.

will continue to appear to the individual in the waking and dream states as long as there are latent mental impressions. Just as the lens magnifies the tiny specks on the film to a huge size and as a number of pictures are shown in a second, so the mind enlarges the sprout-like tendencies into tree-like thoughts and shows in a second innumerable worlds. Again, just as there is only the light of the lamp visible when there is no film, so the Self alone shines without the triple factors when the mental concepts in the form of tendencies are absent in the states of deep sleep, swoon and *samadhi*. Just as the lamp illumines the lens, etc., while remaining unaffected, the Self illumines the ego (*chidabhasa*), etc., while remaining unaffected.

14. *What is* dhyana *(meditation)?*

It is abiding as one's Self without swerving in any way from one's real nature and without feeling that one is meditating. As one is not in the least conscious of the different states (waking, dreaming, etc.) in this condition, the sleep (noticeable) here is also regarded as *dhyana*.

15. *What is the difference between* dhyana *and* samadhi?

Dhyana is achieved through deliberate mental effort; in *samadhi* there is no such effort.

16. *What are the factors to be kept in view in* dhyana?

It is important for one who is established in his Self (*atma nishta*) to see that he does not swerve in the least from this absorption. By swerving from his true nature he may see before him bright effulgences, etc., or hear (unusual) sounds or regard as real the visions of gods appearing within or outside himself. He should not be deceived by these and forget himself.

Note: (i) If the moments that are wasted in thinking of the objects which are not the Self, are spent on enquiry into the Self, Self-realization will be attained in a very short time.

(ii) Until the mind becomes established in itself some kind of bhavana *(contemplation of a personified god or goddess with deep emotion and religious feeling) is essential. Otherwise the mind will be frequently assailed by wayward thoughts or sleep.*

(iii) Without spending all the time in practising bhavanas *like 'I am Siva' or 'I am* Brahman*', which are regarded as* nirgunopasana *(contemplation of the attributeless* Brahman*), the method of enquiry into oneself should be practised as soon as the mental strength which is the result of such* upasana *(contemplation) is attained.*

The excellence of the practice (sadhana) *lies in not giving room for even a single mental concept* (vritti).

17. *What are the rules of conduct which an aspirant* (sadhaka) *should follow?*

Moderation in food, moderation in sleep and moderation in speech.

18. *How long should one practise?*

Until the mind attains effortlessly its natural state of freedom from concepts, that is till the sense of 'I' and 'mine' exists no longer.

19. *What is the meaning of dwelling in solitude* (ekanta vasa)?

As the Self is all-pervasive it has no particular place for solitude. The state of being free from mental concepts is called 'dwelling in solitude'.

20. *What is the sign of wisdom* (viveka)?

Its beauty lies in remaining free from delusion after realising the truth once. There is fear only for one who sees at least a slight difference in the Supreme *Brahman*. So long as there is the idea that the body is the Self one cannot be a realizer of truth whoever he might be.

21. *If everything happens according to* karma *(prarabdha, the result of one's acts in the past) how is one to overcome the obstacles to meditation* (dhyana)?

Prarabdha concerns only the out-turned, not the in-turned mind. One who seeks his real Self will not be afraid of any obstacle.

22. *Is asceticism* (sannyasa) *one of the essential requisites for a person to become established in the Self* (atma nishta)?

The effort that is made to get rid of attachment to one's body is really towards abiding in the Self. Maturity of thought and enquiry alone removes attachment to the body, not the stations of life (*ashramas*), such as student (*brahmachari*), etc. For the attachment is in the mind while the stations pertain to the body. How can bodily stations remove the attachment in the mind? As maturity of thought and enquiry pertain to the mind these alone can, by enquiry on the part of the same mind, remove the attachments which have crept into it through thoughtlessness. But, as the discipline of asceticism (*sannyasashrama*) is the means for attaining dispassion (*vairagya*), and as dispassion is the means for enquiry, joining an order of ascetics may be regarded, in a way, as a means of enquiry through dispassion. Instead of wasting one's life by entering the order of ascetics before one is fit for it, it is better to live the householder's life. In order to fix the mind in the Self which is its true nature it is necessary to separate it from the family of fancies (*sankalpas*) and doubts (*vikalpas*), that is to renounce the family (*samsara*) in the mind. This is real asceticism.

23. *It is an established rule that so long as there is the least idea of I-am-the-doer, Self-knowledge cannot be attained, but is it possible for an aspirant who is a householder to discharge his duties properly without this sense?*

As there is no rule that action should depend upon a sense of being the doer it is unnecessary to doubt whether any action will take place without a doer or an act of doing. Although the officer of a government treasury may appear, in the eyes of others, to be doing his duty attentively and responsibly all day long, he will be discharging his duties without attachment, thinking 'I have no real connection with all this money' and without a sense of involvement in his mind. In the same manner a wise householder may also discharge without attachment the various household duties which fall to his lot according to his past *karma*, like a tool in the hands of another. Action and knowledge are not obstacles to each other.

24. *Of what use to his family is a wise householder who is unmindful of his bodily comforts and of what use is his family to him?*

Although he is entirely unmindful of his bodily comforts, if, owing to his past *karma*, his family have to subsist by his efforts, he may be regarded as doing service to others. If it is asked whether the wise man derives any benefit from the discharge of domestic duties, it may be answered that, as he has already attained the state of complete satisfaction which is the sum total of all benefits and the highest good of all, he does not stand to gain anything more by discharging family duties.

25. *How can cessation of activity* (nivritti) *and peace of mind be attained in the midst of household duties which are of the nature of constant activity?*

As the activities of the wise man exist only in the eyes of others and not in his own, although he may be accomplishing immense tasks, he really does nothing. Therefore his activities do not stand in the way of inaction and peace of mind. For he knows the truth that all activities take place in his mere presence and that he does nothing. Hence he will remain as the silent witness of all the activities taking place.

26. *Just as the sage's past* karma *is the cause of his present activities will not the impressions* (vasanas) *caused by his present activities adhere to him in future?*

Only one who is free from all the latent tendencies (*vasanas*) is a sage. That being so how can the tendencies of *karma* affect him who is entirely unattached to activity?

27. *What is the meaning of* brahmacharya?

Only enquiry into *Brahman* should be called *brahmacharya.*

28. *Will the practice of* brahmacharya *which is followed in conformity with the (four) orders of life* (ashramas) *be a means of knowledge?*

As the various means of knowledge, such as control of senses, etc., are included in *brahmacharya* the virtuous practices duly followed by those who belong to the order of students (*brahmacharins*) are very helpful for their improvement.

29. *Can one enter the order of ascetics* (sanyasa) *directly from the order of students* (brahmacharya)?

Those who are competent need not formally enter the orders of *brahmacharya*, etc., in the order laid down. One who has realized his Self does not distinguish between the various orders of life. Therefore no order of life either helps or hinders him.

30. *Does an aspirant* (sadhaka) *lose anything by not observing the rules of caste and orders of life?*

As the attainment (*anusthana, lit.* practice) of knowledge is the supreme end of all other practices, there is no rule that one who remains in any one order of life and constantly acquires knowledge is bound to follow the rules laid down for that order of life. If he follows the rules of caste and orders of life he does so for the good of the world. He does not derive any benefit by observing the rules. Nor does he lose anything by not observing them.

CHAPTER III

EXPERIENCE
(*Anubhava*)

1. *What is the light of consciousness?*

It is the self-luminous existence-consciousness which reveals to the seer the world of names and forms both inside and outside. The existence of this existence-consciousness can be inferred by the objects illuminated by it. It does not become the object of consciousness.

2. *What is knowledge* (vijnana)?

It is that tranquil state of existence-consciousness which is experienced by the aspirant and which is like the waveless ocean or the motionless ether.

3. *What is bliss?*

It is the experience of joy (or peace) in the state of *vijnana* free of all activities and similar to deep sleep. This is also called the state of *kevala nirvikalpa* (remaining without concepts).

4. *What is the state beyond bliss?*

It is the state of unceasing peace of mind which is found in the state of absolute quiescence, *jagrat-sushupti* (*lit.* sleep with awareness) which resembles inactive deep sleep. In this state, in spite of the activity of the body and the senses, there is no external awareness, like a child immersed in sleep[1] (who is not conscious of the food given to him by his mother). A *yogi* who is in this state is inactive even while engaged in activity.

---

[1] The acts of sleeping children like eating and drinking are acts only in the eyes of others and not in their own. They do not therefore really do those acts in spite of their appearing to do them.

This is also called *sahaja nirvikalpa samadhi* (natural state of absorption in oneself without concepts).

5. *What is the authority for saying that the entire moving and unmoving worlds depend upon oneself?*

The Self means the embodied being. It is only after the energy, which was latent in the state of deep sleep, emerges with the idea of 'I' that all objects are experienced. The Self is present in all perceptions as the perceiver. There are no objects to be seen when the 'I' is absent. For all these reasons it may undoubtedly be said that everything comes out of the Self and goes back to the Self.

6. *As the bodies and the selves animating them are everywhere actually observed to be innumerable how can it be said that the Self is only one?*

If the idea 'I am the body' is accepted[2], the selves are multiple. The state in which this idea vanishes is the Self, since in that state there are no other objects. It is for this reason that the Self is regarded as one only.

7. *What is the authority for saying that* Brahman *can be apprehended by the mind and at the same time that it cannot be apprehended by the mind?*

It cannot be apprehended by the impure mind but can be apprehended by the pure mind.

8. *What is pure mind and what is impure mind?*

When the indefinable power of *Brahman* separates itself from *Brahman* and, in union with the reflection of consciousness (*chidabhasa*) assumes various forms, it is called the impure mind. When it becomes free from the reflection of consciousness

---

[2] The idea that one is one's body is what is called *hrdaya-granthi* (knot of the heart). Of the various knots, this one, which binds together what is conscious with what is insentient, is what causes bondage.

(*abhasa*), through discrimination, it is called the pure mind. Its state of union with the *Brahman* is its apprehension of *Brahman*. The energy which is accompanied by the reflection of consciousness is called the impure mind and its state of separation from *Brahman* is its non-apprehension of *Brahman*.

9. *Is it possible to overcome, even while the body exists, the* karma (prarabdha) *which is said to last till the end of the body?*

Yes. If the agent (doer) upon whom the *karma* depends, namely the ego, which has come into existence between the body and the Self, merges in its source and loses its form, will the *karma* which depends upon it alone survive? Therefore when there is no 'I' there is no *karma*.

10. *As the Self is existence and consciousness, what is the reason for describing it as different from the existent and the non-existent, the sentient and the insentient?*

Although the Self is real, as it comprises everything, it does not give room for questions involving duality about its reality or unreality. Therefore it is said to be different from the real and the unreal. Similarly, even though it is consciousness, since there is nothing for it to know or to make itself known to, it is said to be different from the sentient and the insentient.

CHAPTER IV

ATTAINMENT
(Arudha)

1. *What is the state of attainment of knowledge?*

It is firm and effortless abidance in the Self in which the mind which has become one with the Self does not subsequently emerge again at any time. That is, just as everyone usually and naturally has the idea, 'I am not a goat nor a cow nor any other animal but a human', when he thinks of his body, so also when he has the idea 'I am not the principles (*tattwas*) beginning with the body and ending with sound (*nada*), but the Self which is existence, consciousness and bliss, the innate self-consciousness (*atma prajna*)', he is said to have attained firm knowledge.

2. *To which of the seven stages of knowledge* (jnana bhoomikas)[1] *does the sage* (jnani) *belong?*

He belongs to the fourth stage.

3. *If that is so why have three more stages superior to it been distinguished?*

The marks of the stages four to seven are based upon the experiences of the realized person (*jivanmukta*). They are not states of knowledge and release. So far as knowledge and release are concerned no distinction whatever is made in these four stages.

---

[1] The seven *jnana bhoomikas* are:

1. *subheccha* (the desire for enlightenment).
2. *vicharana* (enquiry).
3. *tanumanasa* (tenuous mind).
4. *satwapatti* (self-realization).
5. *asamsakti* (non-attachment).
6. *padarthabhavana* (non-perception of objects).
7. *turyaga* (transcendence).

Those who have attained the last four *bhoomikas* are called *brahmavit, brahmavidvara, brahmavidvariya* and *brahmavid varistha* respectively.

4. *As liberation is common to all, why is the* varistha *(lit. the most excellent) alone praised excessively?*

So far as the *varistha's* common experience of bliss is concerned he is extolled only because of the special merit acquired by him in his previous births which is the cause of it.

5. *As there is no one who does not desire to experience constant bliss what is the reason why all sages* (jnanis) *do not attain the state of* varistha?

It is not to be attained by mere desire or effort. *Karma* (*prarabdha*) is its cause. As the ego dies along with its cause even in the fourth stage (*bhoomika*), what agent is there beyond that stage to desire anything or to make efforts? So long as they make efforts they will not be sages (*jnanis*). Do the sacred texts (*srutis*) which specially mention the *varistha* say that the other three are unenlightened persons?

6. *As some sacred texts say that the supreme state is that in which the sense organs and the mind are completely destroyed, how can that state be compatible with the experience of the body and the senses?*

If that were so there would not be any difference between that state and the state of deep sleep. Further, how can it be said to be the natural state when it exists at one time and not at another? This happens, as stated before, to some persons according to their *karma (prarabdha)* for some time or till death. It cannot properly be regarded as the final state. If it could it would mean that all great souls and the Lord, who were the authors of the *Vedantic* works *(jnana granthas)* and the Vedas, were unenlightened persons. If the supreme state is that in which neither the senses nor the mind exist and not the state in which they exist, how can it be the perfect state (*paripurnam*)? As *karma* alone is responsible for the activity or inactivity of the sages, great souls have declared the state of *sahaja nirvikalpa* (the natural state without concepts) alone to be the ultimate state.

7. *What is the difference between ordinary sleep and waking sleep* (jagrat sushupti)?

In ordinary sleep there are not only no thoughts but also no awareness. In waking sleep there is awareness alone. That is why it is called awake while sleeping, that is the sleep in which there is awareness.

8. *Why is the Self described both as the fourth state* (turiya) *and beyond the fourth state* (turiyatita)?

Turiya means that which is the fourth. The experiencers (*jivas*) of the three states of waking, dreaming and deep sleep, known as *visva, taijasa* and *prajna*, who wander successively in these three states, are not the Self. It is with the object of making this clear, namely that the Self is that which is different from them and which is the witness of these states, that it is called the fourth *(turiya)*. When this is known, the three experiencers disappear and the idea that the Self is a witness, that it is the fourth, also disappears. That is why the Self is described as beyond the fourth *(turiyatita)*.

9. *What is the benefit derived by the sage from the sacred books* (srutis)?

The sage who is the embodiment of the truths mentioned in the scriptures has no use for them.

10. *Is there any connection between the attainment of supernatural powers* (siddhis) *and liberation* (mukti)?

Enlightened enquiry alone leads to liberation. Supernatural powers are all illusory appearances created by the power of *maya* (*mayashakti*). Self-realization which is permanent is the only true accomplishment (*siddhi*). Accomplishments which appear and disappear, being the effect of *maya*, cannot be real. They are accomplished with the object of enjoying fame, pleasures, etc. They come unsought to some persons through their *karma*. Know that union with *Brahman* is the real aim of all accomplishments.

This is also the state of liberation (*aikya mukti*) known as union (*sayujya*).

11. *If this is the nature of liberation* (moksha) *why do some scriptures connect it with the body and say that the individual soul can attain liberation only when it does not leave the body?*

It is only if bondage is real that liberation and the nature of its experiences have to be considered. So far as the Self (*Purusha*) is concerned it has really no bondage in any of the four states. As bondage is merely a verbal assumption according to the emphatic proclamation of the *Vedanta* system, how can the question of liberation, which depends upon the question of bondage, arise when there is no bondage? Without knowing this truth, to enquire into the nature of bondage and liberation, is like enquiring into the non-existent height, colour, etc., of a barren woman's son or the horns of a hare.

12. *If that is so, do not the descriptions of bondage and release found in the scriptures become irrelevant and untrue?*

No, they do not. On the contrary, the delusion of bondage fabricated by ignorance from time immemorial can be removed only by knowledge, and for this purpose the term 'liberation' (*mukti*) has been usually accepted. That is all. The fact that the characteristics of liberation are described in different ways proves that they are imaginary.

13. *If that is so, are not all efforts such as study (lit. hearing) reflection, etc., useless?*

No, they are not. The firm conviction that there is neither bondage nor liberation is the supreme purpose of all efforts. As this purpose of seeing boldly, through direct experience, that bondage and liberation do not exist, cannot be achieved except with the aid of the aforesaid practices, these efforts are useful.

14. *Is there any authority for saying that there is neither bondage*
    nor liberation?

This is decided on the strength of experience and not
merely on the strength of the scriptures.

15. *If it is experienced how is it experienced?*

'Bondage' and 'liberation' are mere linguistic terms.
They have no reality of their own. Therefore they cannot
function of their own accord. It is necessary to accept the
existence of some basic thing of which they are the
modifications. If one enquires, 'for whom is there bondage
and liberation?' it will be seen, 'they are for me'. If one
enquires, 'Who am I?', one will see that there is no such
thing as the 'I'. It will then be as clear as an *amalaka* fruit in
one's hand that what remains is one's real being. As this truth
will be naturally and clearly experienced by those who leave
aside mere verbal discussions and enquire into themselves
inwardly, there is no doubt that all realized persons uniformly
see neither bondage nor liberation so far as the true Self is
concerned.

16. *If truly there is neither bondage nor liberation what is the*
    reason for the actual experience of joys and sorrows?

They appear to be real only when one turns aside from
one's real nature. They do not really exist.

17. *Is it possible for everyone to know directly without doubt what*
    exactly is one's true nature?

Undoubtedly it is possible.

18. *How?*

It is the experience of everyone that even in the states of
deep sleep, fainting, etc., when the entire universe, moving and
stationary, beginning with earth and ending with the
unmanifested *(prakriti)*, disappear, he does not disappear.
Therefore the state of pure being which is common to all and

which is always experienced directly by everybody is one's true nature. The conclusion is that all experiences in the enlightened as well as the ignorant state, which may be described by newer and newer words, are opposed to one's real nature.

May this book consisting of the words of experience, which have come out of the lotus heart of Bhagavan Sri Ramana Maharshi, shine as a lamp of true knowledge to illuminate the true minds of those who have renounced (the world).

BLESSINGS

May the world be blessed for long with the feet of Guru Ramana who abides as that silent principle which absorbs all of us and remains by itself as the root of the three principles (soul, world and Iswara).

OM TAT SAT